THE OFFICIAL
Arsenal
ANNUAL
2003

Written by
Damian Hall

g

A Grange Publication

Published by Grange Communications Ltd., Edinburgh.
™ & © 2002 The Arsenal Football Club plc.
Licensed by Granada Commercial Ventures
Printed in the EU.

ISBN 1-902704-30-4

CONTENTS

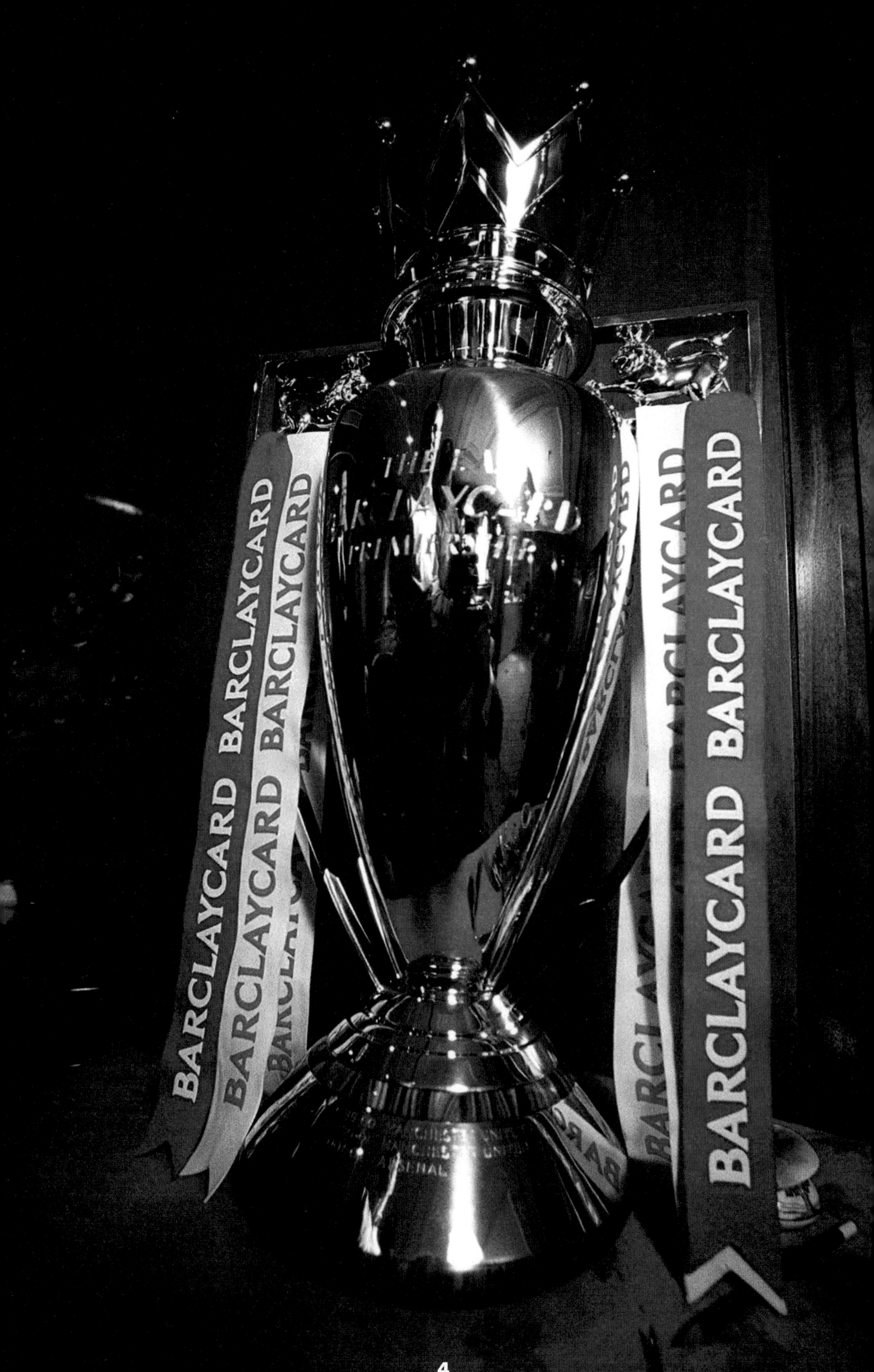
BARCLAYCARD

The Trophy Cabinet

LEAGUE CHAMPIONS (12 times):

1931, 1933, 1934, 1935, 1938, 1948, 1953, 1971, 1989, 1991, 1998, 2002
Runners-Up: 1926, 1932, 1973, 1999, 2000, 2001

F.A. CUP WINNERS (8 times):

1930, 1936, 1950, 1971, 1979, 1993, 1998, 2002
Runners-Up: 1927, 1932, 1952, 1972, 1978, 1980, 2001

LEAGUE CUP WINNERS:

1987, 1993
Runners-Up: 1968, 1969, 1988

EUROPEAN INTER-CITIES' FAIRS CUP/UEFA CUP WINNERS:

1970
Runners-Up: 2000

EUROPEAN CUP WINNERS CUP WINNERS:

1994
Runners-Up: 1980, 1995

F.A.YOUTH CUP WINNERS:

1966, 1971, 1988, 1994, 2000, 2001

TONY ADAMS
TRIBUTE TO A LEGEND

At 35, Tony Adams has reluctantly decided to retire from playing football. It is, quite simply, the end of an era - often glorious, always eventful, highly memorable.

To many, Adams was known as 'Mr Arsenal' and his influence at Highbury over the last twenty years can not be overstated. He is not only Arsenal's youngest ever skipper, given the armband by George Graham at a fearless 21, he is also Arsenal's most successful ever. The centre-back has also captained England on 15 occasions, including the 1996 European Championships where Terry Venables' team went out at the semi-final stage on penalties. Not forgetting that Adams has won the league Championship with the Gunners in three different decades (1989, 1991, 1998, 2002). A feat unequalled in English football. In fact Arsenal's Captain Fantastic has worn the armband for every team he's played for – look up 'born leader' in the footballing dictionary and there's a picture of him.

Branded "Captain Colossus" (meaning someone who's so important to the cause that he's larger than life) by Graham, only David O'Leary has played more games for the Gunners in the history of Arsenal Football Club. A quick glance at his career statistics will tell you he's a winner through and through. Making his debut aged just 17 in 1983, Adams spent his entire career at Highbury. In 1987 Adams collected his first of 66 international caps at the age of 20 and was voted PFA Young player of the Year the same season. Adams The Lion Heart went on to lead his team to four League Championships, two League Cups, three FA Cup wins and a European Cup Winners Cup triumph, along with many other finals. His 49 goals is an impressive record for a defender, many were crucial strikes too.

Arsenal fans love him first and foremost because he's an Arsenal man through and through, a 100-percenter whose commitment, belief and resolve have never been questioned. Legend has it that if you dissected his heart (though it wouldn't be too wise to try it) you'd find the Arsenal crest imprinted there.

Granted an emotional testimonial against Celtic in the summer, Adams' next moves are uncertain. But the red side of north London will be hoping he stays at Highbury in some role, to pass on his unique footballing knowledge. The rest of football will probably be hoping he doesn't. Arsène Wenger summed him up neatly. "To find a replacement for Tony at club level is impossible," said the man who also claimed Adams was 'the Professor of Defence'. "He is a one-off."

BARCLAYCARD
PREMIERSHIP
CHAMPIONS
Arsenal
BARCLAYCARD
CLAYCARD

ARSENAL 2001/02
WHEN THE MAGIC WORKED

Phew! What a wonderful season. It had it all. There were moments of spellbinding drama, where tension came close to suffocation; none more so than the nerve-shredding, climactic encounter with Manchester United at Old Trafford, as well as the three games (Ipswich, West Ham, Bolton) leading up to that historic night.

There were some unforgettable moments of divine individual brilliance; Dennis Bergkamp's unthinkably clever goal against Newcastle, Ray Parlour's screamer in the FA Cup final and just about every time Robert Pires touched the ball. There were too some moments of stubborn, dogged, resilient defending when The Gunners' rearguard, and often the whole team, dug in and fought tooth and nail for the rewards they felt they deserved. Again in evidence was the typical Arsenal backs-to-the-wall fighting spirit whenever it was needed most, an asset carefully crafted by a Mr Arsène Wenger. And, most importantly, it was a victorious, glorious season, which will be talked, written and sung about for many many more years to come.

The 2001-02 season was a campaign when Arsenal not only won the Premiership and FA Cup double, a record-equalling third time, but did so with style, flair and a burning hunger made to glow from "all those oh so nears" in recent years.

Arsenal scored in every single league match, a new record. They went unbeaten away from home, a feat not managed since 1889. Not forgetting that Arsenal have the Football Writers' Player of the Year in Pires, the Barclaycard Player of the Year in Freddie Ljungberg, the Premiership's top goalscorer in Thierry Henry and the scorer of the Goal of the Season in Bergkamp. Oh, and not to feel left out the Arsenal Ladies team won their league too.

The ultimate glory lies with Arsène Wenger, 'The Professor', a man who commands worldwide respect for the all-out attacking football he tutors, the polite passion he oozes and refreshing freethinking.

Pull up a chair, put the kettle on, sit back, remember and celebrate the players and the matches from a truly phenomenal year for Arsenal fans everywhere. Ooh to, ooh to be, ooh to be a, Gooner...

DIARY OF A DOUBLE WINNING SEASON

The saying 'start as you mean to go on' has rarely been more relevant than when comparing Arsenal's last two seasons. In August 2000-01 Wenger's team returned from Sunderland having outplayed them, but with a 0-1 defeat. The season ended trophy-less, with a sense of frustrated underachievement.

Last season however, the opening fixture saw an emphatic 4-0 victory over Middlesbrough and the season ended in glory as the Gunners won the Premiership and FA Cup double in sensational, swashbuckling style. The key was their away from and a hunger fed by the familiarity of coming second.

A team with renewed self-belief played with a greater sense of adventure away from home, which produced more goals. More goals brought more wins, which spiralled into greater confidence, even more victories and ultimately two nice big shining pieces of silverware, the Premiership Trophy and the FA Cup. Arsenal's third glorious double and a place in the history books.

AUGUST

P3 W2 D0 L1 F9 A2

The Middlesbrough victory was achieved courtesy of a delicious Thierry Henry volley, an own goal and two clinical strikes from Dennis 'The IceMan' Bergkamp. But it was back to earth with a bump two days later as the Gunners surprisingly lost 2-1 at home to Leeds. Arsenal took this minor setback on the chin however and four days later treated the Highbury faithful to a four-goal feast as they tore Leicester apart, seemingly without breaking sweat. Deadly French duo Henry and Wiltord both bagged their second goals of the season whilst Freddie Ljungberg and Kanu weighed in too.

2001-02:
A SEASON IN FACTS 'N' STATS

Arsenal scored in 39 consecutive games (the final game of last season and all 38 games this season). Yet another a PREMIERSHIP and CLUB RECORD.

SEPTEMBER

P6 W3 D1 L2 F9 A6

After a 1-1 draw at Chelsea, the Gunners returned from the first European excursion with a 0-1 Champions League defeat to Real Mallorca. Back home and another London derby with Premiership new boys Fulham offering a stern test, but a focused Arsenal performance yielded a 3-1 victory with goals from Freddie, Henry and Bergkamp. Now top of the Premiership, the Wenger Boys awaited the visit of German team Schalke 04. They were dispatched 3-2 thanks to two more goals from the inform Henry. Bolton arrived at Highbury the following Saturday looking to frustrate Arsenal, which they did for 74 minutes until Robert 'Bobby' Pires, in unstoppable early season form, set up new boy Francis Jeffers for his first Gunners goal. But Bolton equalised and Arsenal were left to rue two points dropped. Midweek brought another disappointing European away defeat to Panathinaikos, by one goal to nil. A 2-0 win at Derby lifted spirits somewhat as Henry pounced twice more.

2001-02:
A SEASON IN FACTS 'N' STATS

ROBERT PIRES was voted the Football Writers' Player of the Year. THIERRY HENRY came fourth in the same players' poll.

OCTOBER
P6 W3 D2 L1 F12 A9

Though the Gunners were stuttering slightly at Highbury and away in the Champions League, their dominant away form continued at Southampton as Pires bagged his first of 13 and Henry made it safe. It was time to get revenge on Panathinaikos as the Greeks left north London without any more Champions League points, as Henry (who else?) scored a pair. But fans were beginning to whisper about a 'home hoodoo' as Arsenal again failed to finish off Blackburn at Highbury, despite twice leading. Pires, Bergkamp and Henry all scored in a dramatic 3-3 draw. In Europe however, Highbury was a fortress and Lauren's former teammates Real Mallorca where beaten 3-1, precisely the score they needed to qualify from the first group stage with a game to spare. Bergkamp, Pires and Henry all found the net. At Sunderland the following Saturday stand-in skipper Patrick Vieira missed a potential match-wining penalty, as the score remained deadlocked at 1-1. Kanu snatched his second of the season with a bewitching dribble, before Arsenal old boy Stefan Schwarz scored a scorching 25-yarder. The month ended with an irrelevant 3-1 away defeat to Schakle 04, Wiltord scored whilst Wenger rested several key players.

2001-02:
A SEASON IN FACTS 'N' STATS

In 57 matches (not including the League Cup) Arsenal achieved 20 CLEAN SHEETS (15 in 38 Premiership games) and scored 113 GOALS.

NOVEMBER
P4 W1 D1 L2 F6 A8

November, as Arsenal fans know all too well, is usually a month to dread. As the nights grow colder, so too does the Gunners' form and championship challenges have in the past been horribly and mysteriously derailed not long after Halloween. And all the usual signs were there as Charlton bizarrely defeated Wenger's team 4-2. November 17 brought a short trip up the Seven Sisters' road to the home of Tottenham Hotspur. In a tight contest Pires rocketed home a superb 25-yard curler to take the lead but Gus Poyet sneaked home an equaliser on the stroke of full-time. The second Champions League group stage kicked off with a visit to Spain's Deportivo La Coruna, who beat Arsenal 2-0.

2001-02:
A SEASON IN FACTS 'N' STATS

THIERRY HENRY came runner-up (to Ruud van Nistelrooy) in the PFA Player of the Year Award, whilst ROBERT PIRES came third.

Next up at Highbury were champions Manchester United and though the season hadn't yet reached the halfway mark, this was a vital fixture. Arsenal started with 21-year-old Stuart Taylor making his league debut in goal and he was unable to prevent United from taking a first-half lead, against the run of play. Fans feared the worst. The November curse, it seemed, had well and truly struck again. But the team had different ideas and the Gunners refused to give up, attacking constantly with pace, power and cunning. Their efforts bore fruit as Freddie equalised on 48 minutes. But the team wanted the win they deserved and continued to outplay their opponents. Eventually on 80 minutes a breakthrough came when United keeper Fabien Barthez gifted the ball to his international colleague Henry, who didn't miss. To the North Bank's delight, five minutes later the hapless Frenchman repeated the trick and so did Henry. Arsenal had not only won 3-1 and cured the November blues, but moved from fifth place to third in the league. A very important turning point said Wenger.

DECEMBER

P8 W6 D1 L1 F16 A10

The month started with another away win, this time at Ipswich's Portman Road by two goals to nil. Mid week brought high excitement to Highbury as the Italian giants Juventus came calling in the Champions League. But they were no match for their hosts as first Freddie, then Henry struck against his former club with a vicious freekick. Some Bergkamp magic crowned a memorable evening as he twisted turned and tricked his way past a bemused Juve defence before releasing Freddie to finish. It may have been December already but Christmas still came early for Arsenal fans as Arsène Wenger put his pen to a new contract to keep him at Highbury until 2005 and keep Arsenal fans smiling. Though smiles nearly turned to frowns as his team found themselves 2-0 at home to Aston Villa. Wiltord was thrown into the fray at half-time however and quickly volleyed home. Henry followed up with two more, one after some twinkled-toed trickery by Pires.

Even more important than the Wenger re-signing was news that Arsenal Football Club had the go-ahead to start building a new stadium at Ashburton Grove, hopefully ready sometime in 2005. With an ever-growing fan-base the club has outgrown Highbury and a move is the only option. Director Daniel Fiszman described the local council's decision as "the most important evening in the club's history."

Back on the pitch and a 1-1 draw at West Ham, with Ashley Cole the scorer, was followed by a controversial game at home to Newcastle. Two disputed sending-offs (Parlour for Arsenal, Craig Bellamy for the Geordies) and a contentious penalty saw the Toon Army depart with a 3-1 win. Wenger and his players set out to made amends. This would be there last league defeat of the season. Next up was the journey to Anfield and a game that Wenger would hail, after the win over Manchester United, as "the second turning point of the season." Things looked ominous as an Arsenal side without Vieira was reduced to ten men with van Bronckhorst harshly dismissed. But on the stroke of half-time Freddie was tripped in the area and Henry held his nerve to smack the ball home.

After the break some Pires magic down the left enabled Freddie to stab the ball past Jerzey Dudek from close range, Liverpool grabbed one back and Arsenal clung on to register a first win at Anfield for many years and second place in the league. A freezing cold Boxing day saw Arsenal come from behind to win 2-1 against Chelsea, a first Gunners goal for a delighted Sol Campbell and a Wiltord winner. 2001 ended with another one-nil-down two-one-up. This time a Pires volley made in heaven and a delicate Cole header from a delicious Bergkamp pass earned the three points.

JANUARY 2002
P6 W4 D2 L0 F13 A7

The new year brought a new competition and Arsenal popped round the corner from their London Colney training ground to play Division One's

Watford, leaving with a 4-2 win with goals from Kanu, Freddie, Henry and Bergkamp. A 1-1 with Liverpool followed, as did another Freddie strike. Then another draw, away to Leeds with an equalising goal from Pires. Van Bronckhorst headed home his first goal for the club, with Henry and Wiltord also on target, in a mid week win away at Leicester which helped regain the title-race tempo. Oddly the next opponents were Liverpool (again!) as they visited Highbury with a view to repeat their FA Cup victory from last season. But the Gunners wanted revenge badly and got it with a Bergkamp header, it was a sweet feeling. A mid week away win against a determined Blackburn side was welcome, with two more goals from Bergkamp.

FEBRUARY
P6 W4 D2 L0 F16 A6

A tired looking Arsenal team could only manage a 1-1 draw with Southampton at Highbury as Wiltord hammered the ball home from close range. Super Sylvain bagged another, a bizarre shinned volley, in a visit to Everton's Goodison Park as the Gunners collected another three points and embarked on a remarkable winning streak that would end with Tony Adams lifting the Premiership trophy. Division One's Gillingham battled bravely in a 5-2 home FA Cup win which witnessed Adams' eventual return to first team action, which he celebrated with a goal. The Champions League returned too, as did more misfortune as a hard-fought 1-0 away win at Bayer Leverkusen turned into a 1-1 draw in the final minute. A frustrated Arsenal team promptly returned to north London to defeat Fulham in an emphatic 4-1 win. Bayer Leverkuson's visit to Highbury saw arguably Arsenal's performance of the season as they simply ripped the German eventual-finalists to shreds with a devastating attacking show of power, speed and efficiency. The type of stylish football that was a pure honour to witness, Arsenal were hitting untameable form at just the right time.

MARCH
P8 W5 D1 L2 F12 A5

Next up were high flying Newcastle, still with realistic titles ambitions of their own, away. But a professional Arsenal performance, a Campbell goal

THE GOONER GREATS QUIZ

1. Who is Arsenal's most successful captain of all time (winning the championship in three different decades)?

2. In what year did Patrick Vieira make his Arsenal debut?

3. Who is Arsenal's all time top goal scorer?

4. What subject does Arsène Wenger have a degree in?

5. Who was the last Arsenal player to be voted PFA Young Player of the Year?

6. Who was the last Arsenal player to be voted Football Writers' Player of the Year before Robert Pires?

7. Who was the first manager to win silverware with Arsenal?

8. Who holds the all-time appearances record for Arsenal?

9. Which Arsenal striker won the Golden Boot in 1989 and 1991?

10. Who was the Arsenal captain when they won the 1971 double?

ANSWERS ON PAGE 62

and memorable Bergkamp strike, kept Arsenal in the hunt - now placed second in the table. Pires was back on the scoresheet in a midweek home win over Derby whilst is was back up to Newcastle again for an FA Cup quarterfinal the following Saturday. In a frantic affair Arsenal clung-on to a 1-1 draw courtesy of an Edu goal. With games coming thick and fast an inform Deportivo La Coruna came to Highbury with all guns blazing in the Champions League. At two nil down Henry had a great chance to get back in the match with a penalty, but the Frenchman, usually so consistent in front of goal, misfired. Villa Park was the next away venue for another Arsenal away victory with an Edu goal and a Pires stunner whilst Seaman kept the Gunners in the game with a penalty save. With the Premiership still well within their sights Arsenal went to Turin to try and salvage their Champions League campaign against Juventus. Another Henry penalty miss didn't matter, as other results went against them. Now out of Europe the Arsenal squad upped the

determination levels, there was no way they were going to finish another season empty handed. First out of the way was Newcastle in the FA Cup replay and a swift 3-0 dismissal thanks to Pires, Bergkamp and Campbell the game was effectively over on 50 minutes. Ditto for their north-east rivals, as Sunderland were promptly sent packing when Vieira, Bergkamp and Wiltord had the game wrapped up inside half an hour.

APRIL
P6 W6 D0 L0 F12 A1

April saw no let up as the Gunners steam-rolled forward, swishing Charlton aside in a third 3-0 on the trot. Goals this time from Freddie and two from Henry, all within the first 25 minutes. At this stage of the season Arsenal were simply awesome and with a cold-blooded determination you could see their relentless drive for silverware, like hungry wolves, would not stop until the prey – the championship - was theirs. An ideal time for a north London derby then. With five minutes left, Lauren, as cool as a cucumber that's been in deep freeze for ten years, struck a penalty smoothly home for a vital 2-1 win. There was no rest from high-pressure games as Old Trafford welcomed Arsenal and Middlesbrough for the F A Cup semi-final. An own goal granted them the all-important win. The championship race between Arsenal and Manchester United was now neck and neck and any slip up could prove fatal as Ipswich visited Highbury themselves desperate for points. In a nervy encounter an anxious crowd had to wait until the 68th minute for relief as Freddie's opportunism paid off. He collected another 10 minutes later as Highbury breathed a collective "phew." The same applied three days later as this time an organised West Ham side came to frustrate and again finger nails were nibbled until 77 minutes when up popped that Super Swede yet again to deliver a vital vital strike. Kanu making it certain a minute later. The trick was repeated at Bolton, albeit thankfully, a little sooner, as the man of the moment, Freddie delivered as too did Wiltord. 2-0 up at half-time, that's the way it stayed.

MAY
P3 W3 D0 L0 F7 A3

With two Premiership games remaining, The Gunners could temporarily take their minds away from the ifs and buts of title run-in with the small matter of an FA Cup final in Cardiff's magnificent Millennium Stadium and a tussle with Chelsea. In the baking sunshine a tight, tactical game allowed few chances and by the second half the contest was crying out for a moment of genius to slice through the stalemate. And it arrived. As Ray Parlour picked up the ball, Chelsea's defence backed off sheepishly, he feigned a pass and then let fly with a net-buster that screamed into the top corner. Not to be out done Freddie scored a similarly impressive goal to take the trophy, they should have won last year, back to north London. And now for the Premiership. On a balmy Wednesday evening all Arsenal needed from a visit to Old Trafford was to avoid defeat against United, who could also still win the league. And they did it. Or rather, they did better than that. They beat a highly combative side 1-0, stealing the Premiership trophy from United's own back yard. It was a fantastic feeling as Arsenal fans unveiled a banner, which stated clearly what had happened. It read, 'Old Trafford, Champions section.' Meanwhile, the red side of north London thronged onto the streets, jubilant, ecstatic, triumphant, 'over the moon'... Everton were irrelevantly dismissed 4-3 on the final day of the season, a thirteenth straight win, and Henry securing his Golden Boot with a further two goals. What a season.... And the celebrations continued long long into the summer.

2001-02:
A SEASON IN FACTS 'N' STATS

For his outstanding achievements in football, ARSÈNE WENGER has been honoured with the Legion d'Honneur by his native France. The Legion d'Honneur is France's highest decoration, created by Napoleon Bonaparte in May 1802 and first bestowed on July 15, 1804. It is awarded for gallantry in military action or twenty years distinguished service in military or civilian life for work that enhances the reputation of France through scholarship, arts, sciences, politics or sport. The Arsenal boss has lead the Gunners to the Premiership and FA Cup Double twice in four years.

The A Team Quiz
Questions:

1. Who was Arsenal's top-scorer in the league last year?
2. How many goals did he score?
3. Who made the most appearances as a substitute last season?
4. In which country was Arsène Wenger a manager before he came to Arsenal?
5. Which Arsenal player is a Cameroon international?
6. Which Arsenal player is a Nigerian international?
7. Last season, who played in the most games (including the League Cup) for Arsenal?
8. Which veteran full back retired from football at the end of last season?
9. Who scored The Premiership's Goal of the Season last year?
10. How many Frenchmen play for Arsenal?

The Cup Quiz
Questions:

1. Who scored Arsenal's FA Cup final goals in the 2-0 victory over Chelsea?
2. Arsenal beat Middlesbrough in last year's FA Cup semi-final, but where was the game played?
3. Who scored Arsenal's first FA Cup goal last season?
4. Who scored against Arsenal for Newcastle in last year's FA Cup quarter-final?
5. What year was Arsenal's first FA Cup win?
6. Who was Arsenal's manager at the time?
7. How many FA Cup games have Arsenal lost in the last two years?
8. How many players where on the pitch at the end of the game against Liverpool at Highbury last season?
9. Which team did Arsenal beat in the third round of the FA Cup in 1971 and again in 1993?
10. Which team did Arsenal beat in the 1994 European Cup Winners' Cup Final?

ANSWERS ON PAGE 62

THE HISTORY CLUB

Where it all began...the cannons can be seen on a stained glass window in Woolwich Town Hall

In the early days the crest was not as significant a part of a football club's identity as it is today. Shirts remained plain, unless commemorating a significant match, an F.A. Cup Final for example, and the crest was generally reserved for official headed stationary, matchday programmes and handbooks.

Following Arsenal's move north to Highbury in 1913, it wasn't immediately apparent that the Club would embrace the Woolwich Arsenal legacy and keep the cannon as a recognisable motif. The Club soon became just 'Arsenal', the Great War affected football for four seasons and recommencing in 1919/20 'normal' football took some time to settle. During all of this period there was no sign of a crest as such but, in the first matchday programme of the 1922/23 season, when

In 1888, just two years after the formation of the Club, Arsenal, who were then called Royal Arsenal, adopted its first crest (1). This was based largely on the coat of arms of the Borough of Woolwich. The Club was based in the Borough from its formation until 1913, playing at Plumstead Common; Sportsman Ground; Manor Ground; Invicta Ground and the Manor Ground again before heading across London to Highbury, Islington.

The original badge comprised three columns, which, although they look like chimneys, are in actual fact cannons. The significance of the cannons to the Borough of Woolwich derives from the long military history surrounding the area. The Royal Arsenal, Royal Artillery Regiment and various military hospitals - which still dot the landscape today - were all prominent in the Borough.

The cannons on the original crest were obviously a reference to the military influence in Woolwich and despite the Club's ties with the area being cut 89 years ago, the cannon theme has developed throughout the years and has remained prominent on 'the Gunners' different crests down the years, including the new design.

the Gunners played Burnley, a new club crest (2) was revealed - a fearsome looking cannon, that would have sat proudly in the Royal Arsenal of Woolwich.

As can be seen the vertical cannons have gone with the new design featuring a single eastward pointing cannon. Whoever designed this robust looking weapon saw his handiwork used by the Club for just three seasons however, and for the start of the 1925/26 season, the Gunners changed to a westward pointing, narrower cannon (3) with the legend 'The Gunners' remaining next to it.

The derivation of the narrower cannon has never been officially confirmed, but the cannons on the crest of the Royal Arsenal Gatehouse in Woolwich (4) are uncannily similar to that used as the

OF ARSENAL'S CREST

Gunners' symbol.

This cannon crest remained prominent in the Arsenal matchday programme and other publications for 17 seasons. It changed slightly through the years with the wording eventually disappearing, but, despite being usurped by the *Victoria Concordia Crescit* crest in 1949 it has remained a basic symbol of the Club ever since, featuring on official merchandise and stationery throughout the years right up until the present day.

The *VCC* crest (5), which the new crest replaces has been Arsenal's symbol since appearing in the first new style magazine matchday programme of season 1949/50. It would appear to have been in the minds of the Gunners hierarchy for at least a year prior to this. In the final matchday programme of the 1947/48 League Championship winning season, 'Marksman' (aka Harry Homer), the programme editor of the day, wrote:

"...*my mind seeks an apt quotation with which to close this season which has been such a glorious one for Tom Whittaker, Joe Mercer and all connected with The Gunners. Shall we turn for once to Latin? 'Victoria Concordia Crescit'. Translation: 'Victory grows out of harmony.'*"

(5)

Two seasons later and Arsenal unveiled its new crest which incorporated Marksman's latin maxim. Tom Whittaker explained in the 1949/50 handbook (which also included the new crest) that the Club had been impressed by Marksman's motto and it had now been officially adopted by the Club. The new crest also featured 'Arsenal' in a gothic style typeface, the westward facing cannon, the

Borough of Islington's coat of arms and ermine.

For the past 53 years this crest has remained largely unchanged (6), though at the start of this, 2001/02 season it was 'cleaned up' somewhat (7) for commercial reasons, with a solid yellow replacing the different tones of gold and *Victoria Concordia Crescit* written in a less ornate typeface.

(6)

(7)

The Club's identity has thus evolved over the years and the decision to formulate a new crest (8) in 2002 is two-fold. Firstly, as the *VCC* crest incorporates many separate elements introduced over a number of years, there has been uncertainty surrounding its exact origination. Consequently, the Club is unable to copyright the *VCC* crest. Secondly, it has always been one of the Club's primary objectives to embrace the future and move forward. With a new stadium on the horizon and the Gunners consistently challenging for domestic and European honours, the Club believes that this is the ideal

(8)

Into the future with Arsenal

ALL ABOUT JUNIOR GUNNERS

Junior Gunners is 19 years old this season! Arsenal Football Club set up Junior Gunners to encourage our junior supporters to keep in touch with the Club and become involved with the players. They are the future of our Club. If we capture them as children they will in the future bring along their own children and hopefully their grandchildren.

Membership for this season costs £14 and £18 for our overseas supporters.

When you join Junior Gunners you will receive the following:-

▶ A chance to be Arsenal's mascot – drawn at random
▶ A membership card which entitles members to purchase a reduced priced match ticket (subject to availability)
▶ Birthday card & Christmas card
▶ A colour photograph of our Double Winners
▶ Newsletter – sent to you 3 times a season
▶ Souvenir Pack
▶ Discounted membership to the Travel Club
▶ Various competitions, quizzes and events held throughout the season

If you are not already a member, why not give the Junior Gunners office a call on 0207 704 4160 and they will send you a membership form. Or you can look them up on the Arsenal web site arsenal.com. Email address juniorgunners@arsenal.co.uk.

Junior Gunners office hours are: 9.30am – 5pm Weekdays and up to 15 minutes before kick off on matchdays. So why not come along and join at the counter.

HOW WOULD YOU LIKE TO PLAY FOOTBALL FOR JUNIOR GUNNERS???

On most Saturday home matches Junior Gunners and their sponsors, Affinity Internet, invite along a group of youngsters to Highbury. They could be Juniors from another football club, Juniors from a cricket club or even some youngsters from a local school. They come into our indoor gym, play some friendly football against a group of our Junior Gunners, have some lunch and then come into our Family Enclosure in the West Stand Lower Tier to watch the match in the afternoon. We have some fantastic fun – wouldn't it be brilliant if you could join in??

Well, we have Twenty Places to give away and if you are aged between 7 years and 13 years old, all you have to do is find the five differences in the photographs below and write them down on a postcard and send them to us at the Junior Gunners Department at Arsenal Stadium. All entries should reach us by the end of January 2003.

The twenty lucky boys or girls will be invited along to Highbury for one of our Saturday games towards the end of the season.

Come on don't just sit there – get the postcards out!!!

JUNIOR GUNNERS /AFFINITY AWARDS

At the end of every season we hold at Highbury our very special Junior Gunners / Affinity awards – all our Junior Gunners who have won trophies etc throughout the season are invited along for lunch and to receive their awards and trophies from the players.

THIS SEASON'S WINNERS ARE:-

Two Junior Gunners Alex Quinn and Michael Cobden who helped save their friend Jack Horsfall's life after he fell against a glass door and severed an artery.

Young 10 year old JG Christian Cunningham who, even though he has cerebral palsy, still manages to have a fantastic sense of humour and regularly attends Highbury in his wheelchair.

Thomas Grover was nominated for his bravery with his illness.

Sixteen year old James Lightfoot who, despite having time off from school due to illness, still received an award from school.

Alex Pedley a lad from Cambridge who still manages to play football even though he has a partial amputation of one of his feet due to an accident.

Seven year old Glen Shorey has a condition that affects his co-ordination and balance - his brothers nominated him to show how much they care about him.

Shelby Neat, a Junior Gunner from Herne Bay, has a rare genetic disorder – mum says she copes so well with this she deserves one of our awards.

Ten year old Conor Devine was nominated for his bravery, courage and determination to cope with his illness.

Thomas Rowson from South West London was nominated by his mother Anya. Thomas has really worked hard to overcome his illness.

If you know a Junior Gunner who deserves one of our brilliant awards why not write to Sue Connelly at the Junior Gunners and tell her all about them?

A DAY IN THE LIFE OF A JUNIOR GUNNER

Waking up at 9:00am. I know we've done it, the Double is ours!

Wednesday night, Old Trafford – watching the game on the television, with desperate Man U fans knowing that all we needed was ONE POINT! Winning that game was a fantastic feeling, knowing that at the following game, I didn't need to worry!

After getting ready, putting on my Freddie T-shirt I had specially printed, and eating lunch, my family and I make our way to Finsbury Park, for around 2 o'clock. We park at the usual, ritual spot 'under the bridge' in Tollington Park Road. Usually as we are walking down to the ground we get a phone call from our friends, another Arsenal-crazy family, to say they are on their way and that we'll meet them at the World of Sport in 20 minutes. So we arrive at the World of Sport as the crowds bustle through the tube station, ready and raring to go.

Dad gets into the queue for the programme, '£2.50 yer programme', the stall holder calls. We walk through the crowds, Dad and I slip into the shop, seeing what's on offer as Mum and Lauren wait outside for our friends. We come out as the smell of burgers wafts through the air. I get a small punch on my shoulder from Adam as I realise 'The Reynolds' have arrived. We cross Seven Sisters Road as the crowds fill the streets. The roads are lined with red and white as the Arsenal fans make their way to Highbury – the home of the Champions. '2 bags for a pound', comes the cry from the sweet stall, 'peanuts are roasted, get yer peanuts', and 'get yer Gooner Magazine' are also heard walking through the crowds.

As we make our way into the turnstiles Mum gets our tickets out along with my Junior Gunner card. We walk through and into the ground. My Dad and sister get themselves seated in their seats, with the usual crowd excitedly sitting around. Mum, me and the rest of our friends make our way to our seats, with me smiling like crazy as we are sitting on the front row. By the corner flag, we sit and wait as the players warm up before 3pm arrives. On our seats are flags, with Arsenal Double Winners printed on them.

The players come back onto the pitch as the stadium erupts with noise, chanting 'Champions, Champions, Champions..' Just before kick-off Robert Pires is awarded his Football Writers' Footballer of the Year award. The crowds cheer for Pires as we all sing ' Super, Super Rob, Super, Super Rob, Super, Super Rob, Super Robert Pires!'

As the whistle goes, with the players ready to begin, The Gunners enjoy a great start as Cole sets up Bergkamp for a fantastic 'Dennis style' finish to maintain our brilliant record of scoring every game of the Premiership season. The crowd sings his song, 'walking in a Bergkamp Wonderland'. Everton, then unfortunately come back at us with 2 goals, but who was I to worry ?? We already had the league in the bag! Henry scored the equaliser 3 minutes later. As the players continued to play at ease, the half time whistle went. People walk out to the burger and chip stall downstairs. We all queue walking up to the stairs and down to the Kenco Stall to get our cups of tea. We stand and talk then realise its 4 o'clock, hurrying back to our seats.

Henry scores his second goal of the game, as my friend tells me of how close he is to winning the Golden Boot, just after Jeffers came on as a sub for Parlour. Jeffers had a few chances before finally scoring, as the fans leapt to their feet and he ran around shirt-less!! The match finished 4-3, as Highbury awaited the presentation of the Premiership Trophy. Throughout the whole of the game, we were singing, every song from 'we love you freddie, cos you've got red hair' to 'oh to, oh to be, oh to be a gooner'. The atmosphere was fantastic.

We received lots of red and white balloons to blow up and throw as the players passed by. Fireworks went off as the players came back onto the pitch to lift the trophy. In turn, the players went up to receive their individual medals and lift the cup to the glorious crowds. A special moment came when Robert Pires lifted the cup. The other players, on their knees, bowed down to him, an outstanding player, without a doubt my player of the season. The celebrations continued as the players walked around the stadium, with Lee Dixon giving a big thank you to the Highbury faithful. Champagne bottles were sprayed as the team had their photos taken. The fans then started to leave the ground once they knew the on-pitch celebrations were over. We all met in the usual spot, 'at the wall' ready to go to The Duke. We had a drink in the pub with all the happy Arsenal fans before we moved onto Crouch End, waving our flags, for our traditional end of season curry. The waiters met us with their usual smiles as they had expected us to come. We sat down and had our food, chatting about what a great season we'd had and thinking about how early we had to get up the following morning for the parade of the Champions...............

By Junior Gunner Siobhan Songour ......age 16.

MY EXPERIENCE AS A BALL BOY

My name is Jamie O'Donoghue and I am 14 years old. I have just experienced the best year of my life. I was a ball boy at Arsenal last season 'yes I was there for the Double' and would like to share with you how that dream came true.

I have been a Junior Gunner for many years and have been lucky to attend home matches with my parents. At the end of season 00/01 there was a message in the programme for junior gunners to apply for being a ball boy / ball girl for the following season. I phoned the office and was sent an invitation to attend an audition. I went to the ground and was introduced to Martin (he looks after all the ball boy / girl squad) and the Junior Gunner office staff. We were put through lots of different training activities like throwing, fetching and catching a ball. We also practised sitting up straight (this was the most important!)

After the training I waited one week to be told if I was in or not. It felt like a lifetime. I was excited and nervous when the letter came to say I had been accepted and I jumped for joy when I knew I was in. My parents were invited to a meeting to meet Sue (the big boss!) to be told what was expected of me. I had one last training day where I met the rest of the ball boy / girl squad and was happy to see friends that I had made on audition day there as well. We were given our kit and a locker. Our kits were to stay at the ground until the end of the season and then we kept them. Our first home match was against Leeds and when I went to my seat in my kit I felt so important. I felt like one of the squad and my head felt as big as the pitch. We lost 2-1, I was gutted but now as part of the squad I couldn't show it.

As the season progressed I made lots of great friends, every match was different. The Champions league gave us the chance to go on to the pitch to shake the flag. We were given different caps and bibs to wear.

After each match we would collect our chairs, wait for the crowd to go and then get changed. Martin would tell us how we were doing and point out anything we might have done wrong. By the end of the season we were professionals!

Watching the players collect the trophies on the last day will be one of my best memories. Being so close to them and knowing I was a part of it will stay with me for life. Other memories are when David Seaman pulled my cap over my face (I was star struck), Shay Given of Newcastle gave me his water and Stuart Taylor always said 'alright boys' and treated us like one of his own.

Thank you Sue, Sharon, Daniel and the rest of the gang for letting me have this experience, I would love to do it all over again. I made some fantastic friends and can't wait to meet up with them at the end of season party, where I will meet all the players and be able to talk with them about my wonderful season at the Arsenal.

P.S If I change my name and put on a disguise do you think I could do it again this year!

GUNNERSAURUS

Did Gunner enjoy last season or wot??? He was absolutely exhausted at the end of the season, there were so many times his nerves were on edge! Every match towards the end was like going to a cup final!!

So during the summer he took it really easy, he had lots of mornings just lazing in his bed, spending his day walking around the pitch, watching the grounds men taking care of our fantastic pitch, sitting in the Northbank with his feet up catching up on his reading.

Now he feels like a brand new dinosaur!!

So on Sunday 11th August the day of the Community Shield against Liverpool when he set off from Highbury at 7am in the morning, he was really looking forward to getting back to entertaining everyone before the matches and of course to see all his friends again.

Gunner arrived in time to see our players arrive at the Millennium Stadium in Cardiff, as they got off the coach he saw there were a few new faces amongst them. It was our new signings Gilberto and Pascal Cygan, Kolo Toure who we signed last season and Jeremie Aliadiere who is now a full first team squad member – I am sure he will get to know them all this season!

Then it was time to go onto the pitch – what a fantastic stadium, the atmosphere at Cardiff is always electric, the stadium was gradually filling up, you could see all the red shirts coming into the stadium, both Arsenal and Liverpool supporters – it was fantastic to see!

Before Gunner did his usual walk around the stadium to meet all the supporters, Gunner went and met George our mascot. George Pummell is 9 years old and comes from Ilford in Essex, George was chosen from all the Junior Gunners who joined before the end of July. He had only been a member for one week!!

George had travelled to Cardiff by train with his family. His father Les came into the Stadium with him when he met Sue from the Junior Gunners office.

Sue introduced Gunner to George and they hit it off straight away! Gunner showed George his new football boots – Gunner is so proud of them! Stuart our Club photographer came over and took some pictures of them both – don't they look smart.

Gunner then went over to see Liverpool's mascot Connor. Connor was in his wheelchair and had a smile as big as Gunners.

Then it was time to go off and see the supporters. How do you think they will like Gunners new kit? He was a bit worried, but there just was no need, everyone loved it, they could not wait until the Gunners Shop had them in stock, so they could all purchase theirs!

Off he started on his walk, shaking hands, waving at everyone – he even went into the crowd on a few occasions to pick the young fans up and have their photograph taken. Gunner arrived back at the tunnel just as the teams were getting ready to come out – Gunner out of the way, no one can get past!! Gunners tummy was really excited seeing all our team in their new kit, Our Club captain Patrick Vieira at the front holding the pennant he would exchange with Sami Hyypia Liverpool's Captain – oh it's great to be back!!

So all in all Gunner really enjoyed his summer off, loafing around and doing absolutely nothing! BUT.....he enjoys it best of all when he is with all his friends on match days.

CLASSIC MISQUOTES

"Despite the rain, it's still raining here at Old Trafford."

Jimmy Hill

"I'll never play at Wembley again, unless I play at Wembley again."

Kevin Keegan

"Well actually we got the winner up there with three minutes to go, but then they equalised."

Ian McNail

"Ian Rush, deadly ten times out of ten, but that wasn't one of them."

Peter Jones

"He hit the post, and after the game people will say, well, he hit the post."

Jimmy Greaves

"I can see the carrot at the end of the tunnel."

Stuart Pearce

"Glenn Hoddle hasn't been the Hoddle we know. Neither has Bryan Robson."

Anon

"For those of you watching in black and white, Spurs are in the all-yellow strip."

Anon

"At the end of the day, the Arsenal fans demand that we put eleven players on the pitch."

Don Howe

"It's Great Britain in the all white strip, with the red and blue V, the dark shorts and dark socks."

Ray French

"We've got nothing to lose, and there's no point losing this game."

Bobby Robson

"Well clearly Graeme it all went according to plan, what was the plan exactly?"

Elton Wellsby

"The only thing Norwich didn't get was the goal that they finally got."

Jimmy Greaves

"Football's football, if that weren't the case it wouldn't be the game that it is."

Garth Crooks

"Don't tell those coming in now the result of that fantastic match. Now let's have another look at Italy's winning goal."

David Coleman

"The last player to score a hat-trick in a cup final was Stan Mortenson. He even had a final named after him, the Matthews final."

Lawrie McMenemy

"I'm going to make a prediction - it could go either way."

Anon

DID THEY REALLY SAY THAT!

THE ARSENAL

Arsenal are proud of their great tradition and do their best to maintain the team's 'one big family' spirit off the pitch too. To this end, many ex Arsenal players are still employed by the club today, lending their expertise in all areas from

4. NAME: DAVID COURT
Current role: Assistant Head of Youth Development
Playing position: Midfield
When: 1962/62 – 1969/70

9. NAME: ALAN SMITH
Current role: Community Soccer School Coach
Playing position: Striker
When: 1987/88 – 1994/95

10. NAME: BRIAN HORNSBY
Current role: Community Soccer School Coach
Playing position: Striker
When: 1972/73 – 1975/76

7. NAME: LIAM BRADY
Current role:
Head of Youth Development
Playing position: Midfield
When: 1973/73 – 1979/80

11. NAME: CHARLIE GEORGE
Current role: Matchday Hospitality Speaker
Playing position: Striker
When: 1969/70 1074/75

8. NAME: PAUL DAVIS
Current role: Academy Coach
Playing position: Midfield
When: 1979/80 – 1994/95

FAMILY TREE

coaching – all the way from the first team down to local school children - to matchday hospitality. It's reassuring to know that the 'Arsenal way' is being passed down from generation to generation. Here are the men doing it...

2. NAME: PAT RICE
Current role: Assistant Manager (first team)
Playing position: Right-back
When: 1967/68 – 1980/81

6. NAME: DON HOWE
Current role: Under-19s Academy Coach
Playing position: Right-back.
When: 1964/65 – 1966/67. Howe was also
Arsenal manager between 1983 and 1986

1. NAME: GARY LEWIN
Current role: Physiotherapist (first team)
Playing position: Goalkeeper (youth team)
When: 1980/81-1981/82

5. NAME: STEVE BOULD
Current role: Academy Coach
Playing position: Centre-back
When: 1988/89-1998/99

3. NAME: KENNY SANSOM
Current role: Occasionally helps
Museum Curator on Stadium Tours
Playing position: Left-back
When: 1980/81 – 1987/88

SUB: 14. NAME: JIMMY CARTER
Current role: Occasional Community
Soccer School Coach and Ex-Pro and Celeb Player
Playing position: Winger
When: 1991/92 – 1994/95

BY FAR THE GREATEST TEAM...

GOALKEEPERS

When you're looking for a man you can depend on to keep clean sheets you won't do any better than having a national hero between the sticks.

England's number one for the last eight years, DAVID SEAMAN has saved his country on numerous occasions, perhaps most famously in the 1996 European Championships. And Big Dave must have a fake birth certificate. At 38, after another superb World Cup, he just keeps on diving about his penalty area like an over-excited, newly born kitten. Likewise in the championship run-in, his return to fitness coincided with Arsenal's excellent form and a saved penalty at Villa Park was as crucial as any. The pony-tailed wonder, who has been frustrating opposition strikers in an Arsenal shirt for 12 seasons now, was rewarded with another one-year contract this summer and shows few signs of his real age.

DAVID SEAMAN
Position: Goalkeeper
Squad Number: 1
Age: 38
Height/Weight: 191cm / 6'3, 83kg / 182lb
Joined Arsenal: 15 May 1990
Arsenal debut: Division One v Wimbledon
(a) 25th Aug 1990 (Won 3-0)
International: England

In reserve Arsenal have STUART TAYLOR. The lanky 21-year old is tipped by many to take over from Seaman, not just at Highbury, but one day for his country too. An England Under-16, 18 and 21 International, the young stopper travelled to the Netherlands with Kevin Keegan's Euro 2000 squad to gain experience of the senior set-up.

The Youth Team graduate has performed superbly for the England U-21s and showed maturity beyond expectations in his ten first team outings last year (just enough to receive a championship medal). The pick of the bunch was arguably his league debut, a vital 3-1 win over Manchester United in which he pulled off a brilliant early save to set the Gunners on the road to victory. Last year Arsenal needed three keepers to see them safely through the season and so when Richard Wright went to Everton for first team football, Wenger quickly pinched FABIAN CARINI from Italian Champions Juventus (on a year's loan with an option of a permanent move). The Uruguayan World Cup star looks like being another inspired signing. Aged just 22, Carini is renowned for his bravery and lightening quick reflexes.

DEFENCE

Arsenal had more defenders in England's World Cup squad than other Premiership club. As well as Seaman, SOL CAMPBELL and ASHLEY COLE both starred in a defence that conceded just three goals in five games, including the spectacular shut-out of pre-tournament favourites Argentina. Both packed their excellent league form and understanding of each other's game in their suitcase to Korea/Japan 2002. The signing from Spurs of CAMPBELL was a massive boost to the Gunners last year, especially around January and February as he remained super stubborn and rock-like at the back whilst his defensive

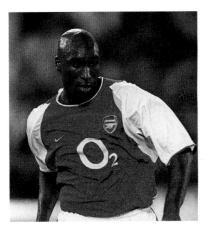

SOL CAMPBELL
Position: Centre-back
Squad Number: 23
Age: 27
Height/Weight: 188cm / 6'2, 83kg / 183lb
Joined Arsenal: 03 July 2001
Arsenal debut: Premiership v Middlesbrough (a) 18th August 2001 (won 4-0)
International: England

comrades changed almost by the week, thanks to horrific injury problems. Having collected twice as many medals in a year with Arsenal as he did in ten years with Tottenham, Super Sol can't have any doubts that he made the right move in the summer of 2001. COLE too excelled with his fearless left-sided raids, even skimming the bar against Argentina. The former forward and Arsenal fan as a boy shackled, shepherded and stopped several of the world's most fearsome strikers, as he doubtless will continue to do for many more years at Highbury. MARTIN KEOWN was as reliable and combative as ever last year swatting away strikers as if they were just mildly annoying flies. The rugged centre-back was rather unfortunate in the

ASHLEY COLE
Position: Left-back
Squad Number: 3
Age: 21
Height/Weight: 173cm / 5' 8", 68kg / 150lb
Joined Arsenal: 24 July 2001
Arsenal debut: Worthington Cup v Middlesbrough (a) 30th Nov 1999 (Drew 2-2) (Boro won 3-1 on pens)
International: England

summer as for the second World Cup in a row he didn't actually get on the pitch. But the fact that three different England managers (Glenn Hoddle, Keegan and Sven Goran Eriksson) have selected him shows how highly the red-booted stopper is rated. First choice at right-back is LAUREN. Also at the World Cup with Cameroon, the athletic African is yet another example of Wenger's remarkable foresight. Arriving at Highbury as a midfielder, his manager has since cast a position-changing spell on him and Lauren now excels as a strong, smooth, attacking full-back. Known to some by his full name Laureano

MARTIN KEOWN
Position: Centre-back
Squad Number: 5
Age: 36
Height/Weight: 185cm / 6'1, 78kg / 172lb
Joined Arsenal: 01 February 1993
Arsenal debut: Division One v WBA (a) 23rd Nov 1985 (Drew 0-0)
International: England

Bisan-Etame Mayer (but more by his nickname 'Ralph') the 25-year-old can also keep a cool head when the pressure's on, slotting home a crucial match-winning penalty in the last few minutes against Tottenham last season. With Arsenal war-horse Tony Adams announcing his retirement, Wenger had to search high and low for the man good enough to replace the almost irreplaceable. And it looks like he may have found him in PASCAL CYGAN. In a seven-year stint with

LAUREN
Position: Right-back/midfield
Squad Number: 12
Age: 25
Height/Weight: 180cm / 5'11, 71kg / 157lb
Joined Arsenal: 30 May 2000
Arsenal debut: Premier League v Sunderland (a) 19th Aug 2000 (Lost 1-0)
International: Cameroon

Lille, he captained the club up from the French Second Division to the Champions League. As yet uncapped by his country, the six-foot three-inch stopper was voted best player in the French First Division by ⫷⫶⫶France Football⫶⫶⫸ magazine in the 2000-2001 season. Left-footed and a good long-range passer of the ball, Cygan is an excellent organiser too. A versatile and valuable squad member, OLEG 'The Horse' LUZHNY can play anywhere across the back-line though his favoured position is right-back. Captain of his country, Oleg tackles like a tank and has previously won six consecutive Ukrainian championships while with Dynamo Kiev. Two more important squad

OLEG LUZHNY
Position: Right-back/centre-back
Squad Number: 22
Age: 34
Height/Weight: 182cm / 6'0, 77kg / 170lb
Joined Arsenal: 28 May 1999
Arsenal debut: Charity Shield v Man Utd (Wembley) 1st Aug 1999 (Won 2-1)
International: Ukraine

members are MATTHEW UPSON and IGOR STEPANOVS. Both centre-backs, Upson offers versatility, a cool head, and high quality passing, whilst Igor, a Latvian international since the age of 19 and the winner of seven league titles with Skonto Riga, provides all the experience necessary for the constant stream of high pressure games Arsenal face all season long.

MIDFIELD

Arsenal's midfield has everything a world class midfield should have, muscle, energy, skill, imagination and goals. Attributes acquired by collecting, and welding together, players positively soaked with world class. Rated by Wenger and Michael Platini (himself considered the best midfielder in the world for much of the 1980s) as the best player in his position in the world, it's no surprise that PATRICK VIEIRA gets linked to every club that could possibly afford him. But the good news is that the supreme warrior-athlete, the club captain and heartbeat of Arsenal's side, is staying. The simple reason? He loves life at Highbury. It's easy to sum up ROBERT PIRES' second season in England. Before it's end he was voted the Footballer Writers' Footballer of the Year 2002. Accolades

PATRICK VIEIRA
Position: Midfield
Squad Number: 4
Age: 26
Height/Weight: 193cm / 6'4, 83kg / 182lb
Joined Arsenal: 14 August 1996
Arsenal debut: Premier League v Sheffield Wed (h) 16th Sept 1996 (Won 4-1)
International: France

don't come much higher than that and put simply the Gallic genius was the Premiership's outstanding player last year as his devastating form sped Arsenal headlong towards silverware. The playmaker doesn't appear to actually run, instead he seems to glide gracefully over the grass, almost ice-skate, as he torments frightened defenders with a feint or a shimmy. Last season the silky sorcerer scored, often important and spectacular, goals with regularity. His flick over a hapless George Boateng and luscious lob over Peter Schmeichel was a close contender for goal of the season. Before he sustained an injury in March 'Bobby' had bagged 13 goals and equalled a Premiership record with 15 goal assists. An incredible talent playing at the peak of his game, and loving every second of it, Pires is on course to

ROBERT PIRES
Position: Midfield
Squad Number: 7
Age: 29
Height/Weight: 185cm / 6'1, 74kg / 163lb
Joined Arsenal: 03 July 2000
Arsenal debut: Premier League v Sunderland (a) 19th Aug 2000 (Lost 1-0)
International: France

FREDDIE LJUNGBERG
Position: Midfield
Squad Number: 8
Age: 25
Height/Weight: 176cm / 5'9, 75kg / 165lb
Joined Arsenal: 12 September 1998
Arsenal debut: Premier League v Man Utd (h) 2oth Sept 1998 (Won 3-0)
International: Sweden

become an Arsenal legend. Next up, FREDDIE LJUNGBERG, whose red gremlin stripe started off a north London craze as old and young, bald and dreadlocked donned the appropriate go faster stripe which also inspired the "We love you Freddie..." song that echoed around Highbury. The would-be punk loves charging like a bull into the penalty area and has a knack of getting crucial goals, his contribution was critical last year when he covered for the absence of Pires. His 17 goals from midfield earned him the Barclaycard Player of the Year award. After a long wait the fans finally got a half decent glimpse of Brazilian playmaker EDU last year. Fully-named Eduardo Cesar Daud Gaspar, the 24-year-old showed himself to be a stylish and clever passer who's attack-minded play meant he scored some important goals for the Gunners in the league FA Cup. The central-midfield man was generally a joy to behold as he played the game with zest and a smile on his face and looks set to play an increasingly important role in Wenger's team this season. Arsenal now have a double dose of Brazilian flair in their midfield with the arrival of World Cup winner GILBERTO SILVA. Wenger's new signing played every minute of every game as Brazil lifted their fifth trophy in

RAY PARLOUR
Position: Midfield
Squad Number: 15
Age: 29
Height/Weight: 178cm / 5'10, 76kg / 167lb
Joined Arsenal: 24 July 1989
Arsenal debut: Division One v Liverpool (a) 29th Jan 1992 (Lost 2-0)
International: England

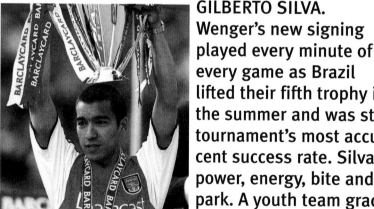

GIOVANNI VAN BRONCKHORST
Position: Midfield/left-back
Squad Number: 16
Age: 27
Height/Weight: 1.86m / 6'1, 71kg / 157lb
Joined Arsenal: 16 January 2001
Arsenal debut: Premier League v Leicester City (a) 2oth Jan 2001 (Drew 0-0)
International: Holland

the summer and was statistically the tournament's most accurate passer, with a 90 per cent success rate. Silva looks likely to bring power, energy, bite and control the middle of the park. A youth team graduate, RAY PARLOUR has always been a tireless runner and a tenacious tackler who plays with greater freedom nowadays, thanks to Wenger's guidance. Making his debut at Anfield in 1992 the curly-haired cannonball was voted Man of the Match when Arsenal beat Newcastle in the 1998 FA Cup final. 'Pele from

EDU
Position: Midfield
Squad Number: 17
Age: 24
Height/Weight: 1.86m / 6'1, 71kg / 157lb
Joined Arsenal: 16 January 2001
Arsenal debut: Premier League v Leicester
City (a) 20th Jan 2001 (Drew 0-0)
International: Brazil (uncapped)

Romford' didn't do too badly in his fourth FA Cup final last season either, as he bagged a screaming solo goal to send the Arsenal fans delirious. Wenger lets him loose in the centre of midfield or as a right-sided flank man and his energy, honesty and power will be priceless as ever this year. His season cruelly cut shot through cruciate ligament injury (the same as Pires) GIO VAN BRONCKHORST will probably still see his first Arsenal season as a slight disappointment. But the neat and tidy midfielder had already proved himself a reliable new addition to the squad. A likeable team-mate, the Dutchman scored his first Arsenal goal at Filbert Street with his head and often filled the left-back slot with ease. Yet to feature in a Premiership game, but most definitely one to watch this year is JERMAINE PENNANT. The 19-year-old right winger is already the youngest ever player to pull on the red and white jersey and has looked confident beyond his years in various League Cup matches. Very fast, very skilful, Pennant looks set for a very bright future indeed.

STRIKEFORCE

What an embarrassment of riches Arsène Wenger has to chose from up-front - Arsenal's arsenal. The main man is THIERRY HENRY, the Premiership's top scorer last season with 23 goals and a man who Sven Goran Eriksson wishes was English. On collecting the Golden Boot HENRY was quick to credit his manager for transforming him from a winger to a striker. A rival to Vieira as Wenger's greatest signing, the sharpshooter is so speedy, so skilful and so lethal. Defenders around Europe must have been having nightmares about him all summer and a disappointing World Cup will only make the 15-year-old hungrier this time around. DENNIS BERGKAMP is Holland's all-time top-scorer and former PFA and Football Writers' Player of the Year (in 1998). Finally fully fit and granted a decent run in the team last season, everything

THIERRY HENRY
Position: Striker
Squad Number: 14
Age: 24
Height/Weight: 188cm / 6'2, 83kg / 184lb
Joined Arsenal: 03 August 1999
Arsenal debut: Premier League v Leicester
City (h) 7th Aug 1999 (Won 2-1)
International: France

clicked gloriously into place for the dynamic Dutchman as he rattled home 14 goals. Among them, the official Goal of the Season, an unthinkably clever strike against Newcastle at St James Park which left everyone drop-jawed in awe. The Iceman is playing like a 19-year-old again and Arsenal fans know how very lucky they are. Super SYLVAIN WILTORD may not have always been first choice in his favoured position as an out-and-out striker last year, but he certainly did his bit for the cause. In fact he appeared in more matches, 54 (in all competitions), than anyone else. The buzzing bumblebee of a player also ended, with Freddie, as the joint second-top scorer with 17 strikes. None were more crucial of course than his championship winning goal at Old Trafford to beat

DENNIS BERGKAMP
Position: Striker
Squad Number: 10
Age: 33
Height/Weight: 183cm / 6'o, 78kg / 173lb
Joined Arsenal: 03 July 1995
Arsenal debut: Premiership v Middlesbrough (h) 2oth Aug 1995 (Drew 1-1)
International: Holland (retired)

Manchester United 1-0 and bring the Premiership trophy back to Highbury, where it belongs. Wiltord, somewhat of an unsung hero, also possesses a tireless work-rate and creative instincts (he made seven goal assists). KANU's is quite some story. Captain of his country, as he was for their historic 1996 Olympics win, the lanky Nigerian has overcome life-threatening heart surgery to continue playing. He's well recovered now and has since set up The Kanu Nwankwo Heart Foundation to help others with cardiac problems. For Arsenal, he is the substitute other managers can only dream of. Wenger often throws him on with 20 minutes left, to showboat

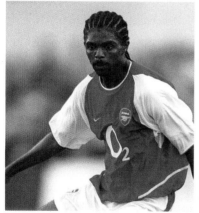

his silky skills and frustrate the opposition. The 2002-03 season could be the season for FRANCIS JEFFERS to really shine in an Arsenal shirt. The small, speedy striker's long-running ankle problems continued to dog him last year. But the scouser has still shown great promise. The boyish assassin has scored two league goals in two league starts and bucket loads for the reserve team, who he turned out for when coming back from injury.

KANU
Position: Striker
Squad Number: 25
Age: 25
Height/Weight: 197cm / 6'6, 80kg / 176lb
Joined Arsenal: 15 January 1999
Arsenal debut: F.A. Cup 5th Round v Sheff Utd (h) 13th Feb 1999 (Won 2-1 but game later replayed)
International: Nigeria

The North London Derby Quiz
TRUE OR FALSE?

1. Between 1991 and 2001 Arsenal met Tottenham in three FA Cup semi-finals. True or false?

2. Robert Pires scored the winning goal in the 2001 FA Cup semi-final. True or false?

3. The aggregate score between the two teams last year was 3-3. True or false?

4. George Graham is the only manager to have bossed the two north London sides.
True or false?

5. Tottenham haven't won at Highbury since 1993.
True or false?

6. Pat Jennings played for Arsenal before he played for Tottenham.
True or false?

7. Tottenham won the league just twice in their history. True or false?

8. Arsène Wenger used to have a Tottenham season ticket. True or false?

9. Tottenham have a former Arsenal player in their squad. True or false?

10. Freddie Ljungberg scored the first goal in the 2-1 over Tottenham at Highbury last season. True or false?

The North London Derby Quiz
TRUE OR FALSE?

ANSWERS ON PAGE 63

ARSENAL WORDSEARCH

The grid below contains 10 names of Arsenal stars and managers of today and yester-year plus words and phrases associated with the club, they are hidden amongst a jumble of random letters. The names may run vertically, horizontally, diagonally, upwards, downwards, forwards, backwards, left-to-right, right-to-left, or any combination of these options.

CAN YOU FIND THEM ALL?

H	R	T	Y	K	C	O	C	A	E	P	T	W	E
B	E	R	T	I	E	M	E	E	L	S	H	R	T
S	G	R	L	T	E	A	E	O	N	K	E	Q	V
L	N	U	B	V	O	O	N	O	B	T	G	B	J
A	E	K	A	E	X	R	I	W	E	J	U	I	Y
R	W	N	J	G	R	P	T	U	G	O	N	R	R
G	E	P	M	Z	M	T	N	M	U	Y	N	S	U
S	N	Q	N	A	A	A	C	G	U	L	E	O	B
O	E	W	H	T	K	E	H	H	B	N	R	S	H
E	S	C	T	O	N	Y	A	D	A	M	S	U	G
T	R	N	A	K	E	V	J	B	J	P	M	L	I
Z	A	A	M	D	E	H	L	F	K	D	M	E	H
R	O	Y	A	L	A	R	S	E	N	A	L	A	A
P	R	U	O	L	R	A	P	Y	A	R	B	F	N

ANAGRAMS QUIZ
Which Arsenal stars, current and former, are these?

Pink German beds
A man did save
Woman tinker
Me penultimate
All banal
Today's man
Up loser man
Ice park trivia
I'm all rigid legs
A dire germ
Cruel banal footballs

ANSWERS ON PAGE 63

PULL THE OTHER ONE
FOOTBALL JOKES

After a visit to the doctor, Joe Bloggs, the city team's centre forward dropped in to his local pub for a quick one. "What's up mate?" asked his friend Brian, "you look worried." "Yes, I am," Joe replied. "I've just been to the doctor's and he told me I can't play football." "Oh, really?" said Brian. "He's seen you play too then, has he?"

Our club manager won't stand for any nonsense. Last Saturday he caught a couple of fans climbing over the stadium wall. He was furious. He grabbed them by the collars and said, "Now you just get back in there and watch the game till it finishes."

It was Cup Final day and a huge crowd was approaching The Millennium Stadium. A funeral procession slowly passed through the crowd. On seeing this; a man took his hat off and stood motionless for a few moments before walking on. "That was a nice thing to do," said his friend. "Well," said the man, "she was a good wife to me for over 20 years."

After considerable effort and expense a First Division manager succeeded in obtaining the services of Miodrag Krivokapic and Mixu Paatelainen of Dundee, Dariusz Wdowczwk of Celtic, Detzi Kruszynski of Wimbledon, and Steve Ogrizovic of Coventry.

"Are these boys any good?' asked a colleague. "I couldn't care less," said the manager. "I just want to get my own back on some of these smart-alec TV sports commentators!"

We Will Remember Him
BERTIE MEE OBE,
Arsenal Manager 1966-1976

Born on Christmas Day 1918, Bertie Mee's playing career as left-winger with Derby County and Mansfield Town was what you might call, in the kindest possible sense, anonymous. Injury forcing retirement at 27, the Nottinghamshire-born man served six years in the Royal Army Medical Corps and from 1948 worked as a rehabilitation officer for disabled servicemen. Having trained as a physiotherapist he joined Arsenal's backroom staff in 1960. Six years later he was the surprise managerial replacement for Billy Wright.

Showing early signs that he was an expert organiser, Mee called in Dave Sexton and later Don Howe to take charge of day-to-day coaching. However Howe, first team coach through the 1970-71 double season, thinks Mee wasn't given enough credit for his football knowledge. "He commanded great respect. In that Arsenal team there were probably six or seven leaders, real men's men. To handle them you had to know your stuff. It wasn't as if he just shut up in the dressing room." The ex-serviceman was also a superb man-manager, often able to tell if a player was having difficulties at home purely from the way he was playing on the pitch.

The Arsenal boss, who commanded a statesmanlike presence around Highbury's marble halls, valued discipline and strong team spirit highly. "He gave you the feeling you were all in it together," remembers Terry Neill. When Mee took charge the Gunners' trophy cabinet had been bare for 13 long years, yet just five years later they were only the second team of the century to win the domestic double. Mee also led Arsenal to the 1968 and 1969 League Cup finals and a dramatic European Fairs Cup win in 1970, coming back from 3-1 to Anderlecht in the first leg to win 3-0 on a memorable North London night.

The 1970/71 double season was remarkable. His team won 11 of their final 13 games to clinch the title at White Hart Lane by a point, whilst in the FA Cup The Gunners were drawn away in every round, coming from behind in the semi-final and final. Mee reached the FA Cup final again a year later and a runners-up spot in the league in 1973. He retired from management in 1976.

Mee later returned to the game to lend his experience at Watford and a young Graham Taylor, who describes him as "one of the best signings I ever made." Mee's wisdom was also in use back at Highbury as George Graham chose to consult him over a cup of tea from time to time. "He was so ahead of his time," said George Graham, "an innovator."

Terry Neill believes he was "in the same class as [great Liverpool managers] Bill Shankly and Bob Paisley." Yet Mee once said, "only the players are important. I am not important." It was a humble thing say. But simply untrue. Mee is an Arsenal legend.

Bertie Mee OBE died aged 82 on Sunday 21st October 2001.

Arsenal

THE SEASON'S TOP THREES:

2001-02 LEAGUE APPEARANCES
(substitute appearances in brackets)
Patrick Vieira 35 (1)
Thierry Henry 31 (2)
Sylvain Wiltord 23 (10)

2001-02 LEAGUE GOALSCORERS
Thierry Henry 24
Freddie Ljungberg 12
Sylvain Wiltord 10

2001-02 FA CUP APPEARANCES
Sol Campbell 7
Patrick Vieira 7
Sylvain Wiltord 6 (1)

2001-02 FA CUP GOALSCORERS
Dennis Bergkamp 3
Freddie Ljungberg 2
Sylvain Wiltord 2
Ray Parlour 2
Kanu 2

2001-02 CHAMPIONS LEAGUE APPEARANCES
Robert Pires 12
Patrick Vieira 11
Lauren 11
Thierry Henry 11

2001-02 CHAMPIONS LEAGUE GOALSCORERS
Thierry Henry 7
Robert Pires 3
Freddie Ljungberg 3

2001-02 OVERALL APPEARANCES
(including League Cup)
Sylvain Wiltord 54
Patrick Vieira 53
Sol Campbell 49
Thierry Henry 49
Dennis Bergkamp 46

2001-02 OVERALL GOALSCORERS
(including League Cup)
Thierry Henry 32
Freddie Ljungberg 17
Sylvain Wiltord 17
Dennis Bergkamp 14
Robert Pires 13

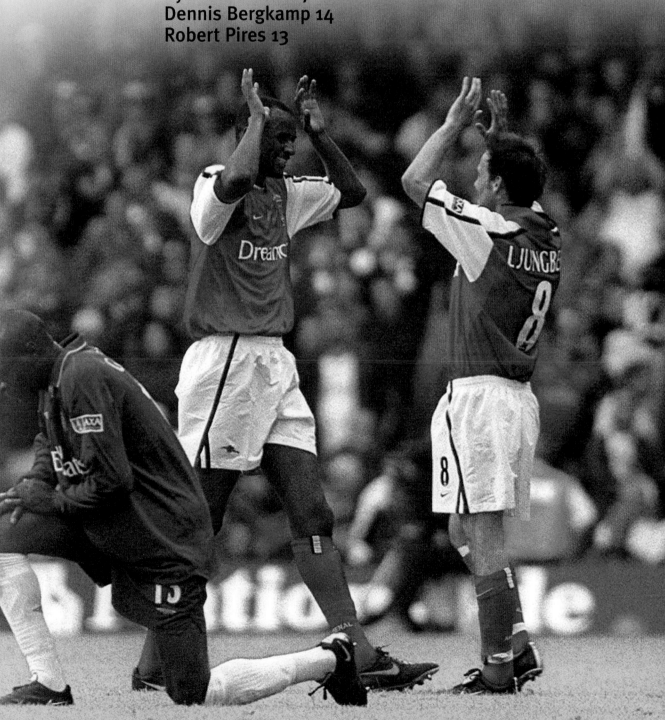

ARSENAL'S 2001-02

AUGUST 2001

Prem Sat 18	A	MIDDLESBROUGH	4	0
Prem Tue 21	H	LEEDS	1	2
Prem Sat 25	H	LEICESTER	4	0

SEPTEMBER

Prem Sat 8	A	CHELSEA	1	1
CL P1 Tue Sep 11	A	REAL MALLORCA	0	1
Prem Sat 15	A	FULHAM	3	1
CL P1 Wed Sep 19	H	SCHALKE 04	3	2
Prem Sat 22	H	BOLTON	1	1
CL P1 Wed Sep 26	A	PANATHINAIKOS	0	1
Prem Sat 29	A	DERBY COUNTY	2	0

OCTOBER

Prem Sat 13	A	SOUTHAMPTON	2	0
CL P1 Tue Oct 16	H	PANATHINAIKOS	2	1
Prem Sat 20	H	BLACKBURN	3	3
CL P1 Wed Oct 24	H	REAL MALLORCA	3	1
Prem Sat 27	A	SUNDERLAND	1	1
CL P1 Tue Oct 30	A	SCHALKE 04	1	3

NOVEMBER

Prem Sun 4	H	CHARLTON	2	4
Prem Sat 17	A	TOTTENHAM	1	1
CL P2 Wed Nov 21	A	DEPORTIVO	0	2
Prem Sun 25	H	MANCHESTER UTD	3	1

DECEMBER

Prem Sat 1	A	IPSWICH	2	0
CL P2 Tue Dec 04	H	JUVENTUS	3	1
Prem Sun 9	H	ASTON VILLA	3	2
Prem Sat 15	A	WEST HAM	1	1
Prem Tue 18	H	NEWCASTLE	1	3
Prem Sun 23	A	LIVERPOOL	2	1
Prem Wed 26	H	CHELSEA	2	1
Prem Sat 29	H	MIDDLESBROUGH	2	1

JANUARY 2002

FA Cup Sat Jan 5	A	WATFORD	4	2
Prem Sun 13	H	LIVERPOOL	1	1
Prem Sun 20	A	LEEDS	1	1
Prem Wed 23	A	LEICESTER	3	1
FA Cup Sun Jan 27	H	LIVERPOOL	1	0
Prem Wed 30	A	BLACKBURN	3	2

RESULTS IN FULL

FEBRUARY

Prem Sat 2	H	SOUTHAMPTON	1	1
Prem Sun 10	A	EVERTON	1	0
FA Cup Sat Feb 16	H	GILLINGHAM	5	2
CL P2 Tue Feb 19	A	B. LEVERKUSEN	1	1
Prem Sat 23	H	FULHAM	4	1
CL P2 Wed Feb 27	H	B. LEVERKUSEN	4	1

MARCH

Prem Sat 2	A	NEWCASTLE	2	0
Prem Tue 5	H	DERBY	1	0
FA Cup Sat Mar 9	A	NEWCASTLE	1	1
CL P2 Tue Mar 12	H	DEPORTIVO	0	2
Prem Sun 17	A	ASTON VILLA	2	1
CL P2 Wed Mar 20	A	JUVENTUS	0	1
FA CUP REPLAY				
Sat Mar 23	H	NEWCASTLE	3	0
Prem Sat 30	H	SUNDERLAND	3	0

APRIL

Prem Mon 1	A	CHARLTON	3	0
Prem Sat 6	H	TOTTENHAM	2	1
FA CUP SEMI-FINAL				
Sun Apr 14	N	MIDDLESBROUGH	1	0
Prem Sun 21	H	IPSWICH	2	0
Prem Wed 24	H	WEST HAM	2	0
Prem Mon 29	A	BOLTON	2	0

MAY

FA CUP FINAL				
Sat May 4	N	CHELSEA	2	0
Prem Wed 8	A	MANCHESTER UTD	1	0
Prem Sat 11	H	EVERTON	4	3

KEY:

Arsenal's score is first on each occasion

Prem – FA Barclaycard Premiership

CL P1 – UEFA Champions League Phase 1

CL P2 – Uefa Champions League Phase 2

FA Cup – Football Association Challenge Cup

Arsenal

FINAL LEAGUE POSITIONS
SEASON 2001 - 02

	Pld	W	D	L	GD	Pts
1 Arsenal	38	26	9	3	43	87
2 Liverpool	38	24	8	6	37	80
3 Man Utd	38	24	5	9	42	77
4 Newcastle United	38	21	8	9	22	71
5 Leeds United	38	18	12	8	16	66
6 Chelsea	38	17	13	8	28	64
7 West Ham Utd	38	15	8	15	-9	53
8 Aston Villa	38	12	14	12	-1	50
9 Tottenham Hotspur	38	14	8	16	-4	50
10 Blackburn Rovers	38	12	10	16	4	46
11 Southampton	38	12	9	17	-8	45
12 Middlesbrough	38	12	9	17	-12	45
13 Fulham	38	10	14	14	-8	44
14 Charlton Athletic	38	10	14	14	-11	44
15 Everton	38	11	10	17	-12	43
16 Bolton Wanderers	38	9	13	16	-18	40
17 Sunderland	38	10	10	18	-22	40
18 Ipswich Town	38	9	9	20	-23	36
19 Derby County	38	8	6	24	-30	30
20 Leicester City	38	5	13	20	-34	28

BARCLAYCARD
PREMIERSHIP
CHAMPIONS

QUIZ ANSWERS

THE GOONER GREATS QUIZ
1. Tony Adams, 2. 1996, 3. Ian Wright (with 185)
4. Economics, 5. Nicolas Anelka, 1999, 6. Dennis Bergkamp in 1998
7. Herbert Chapman, 8. David O'Leary, 9. Alan Smith
10. Frank McLintock

THE A TEAM
1. Thierry Henry, 2. 23, 3. Gilles Grimandi, 21, 4. Japan (Grampus Eight)
5. Lauren, 6. Kanu, 7. Sylvain Wiltord, 54, 8. Lee Dixon
9. Dennis Bergkamp, against Newcastle (a)
10. Five; Patrick Vieira, Robert Pires, Thierry Henry, Pascal Cygan and Sylvain Wiltord

THE CUP QUIZ
1. Ray Parlour and Freddie Ljungberg, 2. Old Trafford,
3. Thierry Henry (Vs Watford), 4. Laurent Robert
5. 1930, Arsenal 2-0 Huddersfield, 6. Herbert Chapman
7. One (the 2001 final), 8. 19 (three had been sent off)
9. Yeovil, 10. Parma

THE NORTH LONDON DERBY QUIZ

1. True (1991, 1993, 2001), 2. True
3. False (it was 3-2 to Arsenal, 1-1 at White Hart Lane 2-1 at Highbury)
4. False. Terry Neill has also, 5. True, 6. False
7. True (1961 and 1951), 8. False, 9. False, 10. True

ARSENAL WORDSEARCH

'Key': ARSENEWENGER, THE GUNNERS, HIGHBURY, HERBERTCHAPMAN, BERTIE MEE, TONYADAMS, CHAMPIONS, ROYALARSENAL, KANU, RAY PARLOUR

ANAGRAMS QUIZ

Dennis Bergkamp, David Seaman, Martin Keown, Emmanuel Petit, Alan Ball, Tony Adams, Paul Merson, Patrick Vieira, Gilles Grimandi, Remi Garde, Arsenal Football Club